Daily Reflections
For the Hero Within

HERO

Title: Daily Reflections
Subtitle: For the Hero Within
Edition Description: Teal Color Cover Edition
© 2025 BEA HERO™
All rights reserved.

Published by BEA HERO™
www.BEAHERO.world

BEA HERO™ is a movement, a publishing imprint, and a lifestyle philosophy dedicated to awakening the Hero within. Through books, coaching, and immersive experiences, we inspire individuals to overcome obstacles, embrace growth, and live with courage, purpose, and contribution.
This journal is part of the BE A HERO: Decode Your Greatness Book — designed to unlock clarity, discipline, and inner power through daily reflection.

ISBN: 978-1-969117-00-8
Cover and interior design by Alessio Favaretto

HERO

Reflections

Date : _____

Emotional Level

- Happy - Peaceful - Relaxed - Energetic - Satisfied - Disappointed - Lethargic - Tensed - Worried - Unhappy -

Things to be grateful for

Today's happiest moments or memories

Today's achievements, or progress

People I am grateful for

Today's quote or best lesson

Tomorrow's goals

Why do I want to achieve it?

How can I best achieve it?

Reflections

Emotional Level

- Happy - Peaceful - Relaxed - Energetic - Satisfied - Disappointed - Lethargic - Tensed - Worried - Unhappy -

Things to be grateful for

Today's happiest moments or memories

Today's achievements, or progress

People I am grateful for

Today's quote or best lesson

Tomorrow's goals

Why do I want to achieve it?

How can I best achieve it?

Reflections

Date : ....

S M T W T F S

Emotional Level

_____ - Happy - Peaceful - Relaxed - Energetic - Satisfied - Disappointed - Lethargic - Tensed - Worried - Unhappy - _____

Things to be grateful for

Today's happiest moments or memories

Today's achievements, or progress

People I am grateful for

Today's quote or best lesson

Tomorrow's goals

Why do I want to achieve it?

How can I best achieve it?

Reflections

Date : ....

 S M T W T F S

Emotional Level

- Happy - Peaceful - Relaxed - Energetic - Satisfied - Disappointed - Lethargic - Tensed - Worried - Unhappy -

Things to be grateful for

Today's happiest moments or memories

Today's achievements, or progress

People I am grateful for

Today's quote or best lesson

Tomorrow's goals

Why do I want to achieve it?

How can I best achieve it?

Reflections

Date : ....

S M T W T F S

Emotional Level

- Happy - Peaceful - Relaxed - Energetic - Satisfied - Disappointed - Lethargic - Tensed - Worried - Unhappy -

Things to be grateful for

Today's happiest moments or memories

Today's achievements, or progress

People I am grateful for

Today's quote or best lesson

Tomorrow's goals

Why do I want to achieve it?

How can I best achieve it?

Reflections

Date : _____

Emotional Level

- Happy - Peaceful - Relaxed - Energetic - Satisfied - Disappointed - Lethargic - Tensed - Worried - Unhappy -

Things to be grateful for

Today's happiest moments or memories

Today's achievements, or progress

People I am grateful for

Today's quote or best lesson

Tomorrow's goals

Why do I want to achieve it?

→

→

→

How can I best achieve it?

Reflections

Date : _____

Emotional Level

- Happy - Peaceful - Relaxed - Energetic - Satisfied - Disappointed - Lethargic - Tensed - Worried - Unhappy -

Things to be grateful for

Today's happiest moments or memories

Today's achievements, or progress

People I am grateful for

Today's quote or best lesson

Tomorrow's goals

Why do I want to achieve it?

How can I best achieve it?

Reflections

Date : ....

S M T W T F S

Emotional Level

- Happy - Peaceful - Relaxed - Energetic - Satisfied - Disappointed - Lethargic - Tensed - Worried - Unhappy -

Things to be grateful for

Today's happiest moments or memories

Today's achievements, or progress

People I am grateful for

Today's quote or best lesson

Tomorrow's goals

Why do I want to achieve it?

How can I best achieve it?

Reflections

Date : _____

S M T W T F S

Emotional Level

_____ - Happy - Peaceful - Relaxed - Energetic - Satisfied - Disappointed - Lethargic - Tensed - Worried - Unhappy - _____

Things to be grateful for

Today's happiest moments or memories

Today's achievements, or progress

People I am grateful for

Today's quote or best lesson

Tomorrow's goals

Why do I want to achieve it?

→

→

→

How can I best achieve it?

Reflections

Emotional Level

- Happy - Peaceful - Relaxed - Energetic - Satisfied - Disappointed - Lethargic - Tensed - Worried - Unhappy -

Things to be grateful for

Today's happiest moments or memories

Today's achievements, or progress

People I am grateful for

Today's quote or best lesson

Tomorrow's goals

Why do I want to achieve it?

How can I best achieve it?

Reflections

Date : ....

Emotional Level

- Happy - Peaceful - Relaxed - Energetic - Satisfied - Disappointed - Lethargic - Tensed - Worried - Unhappy -

Things to be grateful for

Today's happiest moments or memories

Today's achievements, or progress

People I am grateful for

Today's quote or best lesson

Tomorrow's goals

Why do I want to achieve it?

How can I best achieve it?

Reflections

Date : _____

 S M T W T F S

Emotional Level

- Happy - Peaceful - Relaxed - Energetic - Satisfied - Disappointed - Lethargic - Tensed - Worried - Unhappy -

Things to be grateful for

Today's happiest moments or memories

Today's achievements, or progress

People I am grateful for

Today's quote or best lesson

Tomorrow's goals

Why do I want to achieve it?

How can I best achieve it?

Reflections

Emotional Level

- Happy - Peaceful - Relaxed - Energetic - Satisfied - Disappointed - Lethargic - Tensed - Worried - Unhappy - _____

Things to be grateful for

Today's happiest moments or memories

Today's achievements, or progress

People I am grateful for

Today's quote or best lesson

Tomorrow's goals

Why do I want to achieve it?

How can I best achieve it?

Reflections

Date : ....

S M T W T F S

Emotional Level

- Happy - Peaceful - Relaxed - Energetic - Satisfied - Disappointed - Lethargic - Tensed - Worried - Unhappy -

Things to be grateful for

Today's happiest moments or memories

Today's achievements, or progress

People I am grateful for

Today's quote or best lesson

Tomorrow's goals

Why do I want to achieve it?

How can I best achieve it?

Reflections

Date : _____

 S M T W T F S

Emotional Level

_____ - Happy - Peaceful - Relaxed - Energetic - Satisfied - Disappointed - Lethargic - Tensed - Worried - Unhappy - _____

Things to be grateful for

Today's happiest moments or memories

Today's achievements, or progress

People I am grateful for

Today's quote or best lesson

Tomorrow's goals

Why do I want to achieve it?

How can I best achieve it?

HERO

Reflections

Emotional Level

- Happy - Peaceful - Relaxed - Energetic - Satisfied - Disappointed - Lethargic - Tensed - Worried - Unhappy -

Things to be grateful for

Today's happiest moments or memories

Today's achievements, or progress

People I am grateful for

Today's quote or best lesson

Tomorrow's goals

Why do I want to achieve it?

How can I best achieve it?

Reflections

Date : ....

Emotional Level

- Happy - Peaceful - Relaxed - Energetic - Satisfied - Disappointed - Lethargic - Tensed - Worried - Unhappy -

Things to be grateful for

Today's happiest moments or memories

Today's achievements, or progress

People I am grateful for

Today's quote or best lesson

Tomorrow's goals

Why do I want to achieve it?

How can I best achieve it?

Reflections

Date : ....

Emotional Level

- Happy - Peaceful - Relaxed - Energetic - Satisfied - Disappointed - Lethargic - Tensed - Worried - Unhappy -

Things to be grateful for

Today's happiest moments or memories

Today's achievements, or progress

People I am grateful for

Today's quote or best lesson

Tomorrow's goals

Why do I want to achieve it?

How can I best achieve it?

Reflections

Date : _____

Emotional Level

_____ - Happy - Peaceful - Relaxed - Energetic - Satisfied - Disappointed - Lethargic - Tensed - Worried - Unhappy - _____

Things to be grateful for

Today's happiest moments or memories

Today's achievements, or progress

People I am grateful for

Today's quote or best lesson

Tomorrow's goals

Why do I want to achieve it?

How can I best achieve it?

Reflections

Date : _____

 S M T W T F S

Emotional Level

_____ - Happy - Peaceful - Relaxed - Energetic - Satisfied - Disappointed - Lethargic - Tensed - Worried - Unhappy - _____

Things to be grateful for

Today's happiest moments or memories

Today's achievements, or progress

People I am grateful for

Today's quote or best lesson

Tomorrow's goals

Why do I want to achieve it?

How can I best achieve it?

Reflections

Date : ....

S M T W T F S

Emotional Level

- Happy - Peaceful - Relaxed - Energetic - Satisfied - Disappointed - Lethargic - Tensed - Worried - Unhappy - _____

Things to be grateful for

Today's happiest moments or memories

Today's achievements, or progress

People I am grateful for

Today's quote or best lesson

Tomorrow's goals

Why do I want to achieve it?

How can I best achieve it?

Reflections

Date : ....

Emotional Level

- Happy - Peaceful - Relaxed - Energetic - Satisfied - Disappointed - Lethargic - Tensed - Worried - Unhappy -

Things to be grateful for

Today's happiest moments or memories

Today's achievements, or progress

People I am grateful for

Today's quote or best lesson

Tomorrow's goals

Why do I want to achieve it?

How can I best achieve it?

Reflections

Date : ....

Emotional Level

- Happy - Peaceful - Relaxed - Energetic - Satisfied - Disappointed - Lethargic - Tensed - Worried - Unhappy -

Things to be grateful for

Today's happiest moments or memories

Today's achievements, or progress

People I am grateful for

Today's quote or best lesson

Tomorrow's goals

Why do I want to achieve it?

How can I best achieve it?

Reflections

Date : _____

Emotional Level

- Happy - Peaceful - Relaxed - Energetic - Satisfied - Disappointed - Lethargic - Tensed - Worried - Unhappy -

Things to be grateful for

Today's happiest moments or memories

Today's achievements, or progress

People I am grateful for

Today's quote or best lesson

Tomorrow's goals

Why do I want to achieve it?

How can I best achieve it?

Reflections

Date : _____

Emotional Level

- Happy - Peaceful - Relaxed - Energetic - Satisfied - Disappointed - Lethargic - Tensed - Worried - Unhappy - _____

Things to be grateful for

Today's happiest moments or memories

Today's achievements, or progress

People I am grateful for

Today's quote or best lesson

Tomorrow's goals

Why do I want to achieve it?

How can I best achieve it?

HERO

Reflections

Date : ....

 S M T W T F S

Emotional Level

___ - Happy - Peaceful - Relaxed - Energetic - Satisfied - Disappointed - Lethargic - Tensed - Worried - Unhappy - ___

Things to be grateful for

Today's happiest moments or memories

Today's achievements, or progress

People I am grateful for

Today's quote or best lesson

Tomorrow's goals

Why do I want to achieve it?

How can I best achieve it?

Reflections

Date : ....

S M T W T F S

Emotional Level

- Happy - Peaceful - Relaxed - Energetic - Satisfied - Disappointed - Lethargic - Tensed - Worried - Unhappy - _____

Things to be grateful for

Today's happiest moments or memories

Today's achievements, or progress

People I am grateful for

Today's quote or best lesson

Tomorrow's goals   **Why do I want to achieve it?**

How can I best achieve it?

HERO

Reflections

Date : _____

S M T W T F S

Emotional Level

- Happy - Peaceful - Relaxed - Energetic - Satisfied - Disappointed - Lethargic - Tensed - Worried - Unhappy -

Things to be grateful for

Today's happiest moments or memories

Today's achievements, or progress

People I am grateful for

Today's quote or best lesson

Tomorrow's goals

Why do I want to achieve it?

How can I best achieve it?

Reflections

Date : ....

S M T W T F S

Emotional Level

- Happy - Peaceful - Relaxed - Energetic - Satisfied - Disappointed - Lethargic - Tensed - Worried - Unhappy - _____

Things to be grateful for

Today's happiest moments or memories

Today's achievements, or progress

People I am grateful for

Today's quote or best lesson

Tomorrow's goals

Why do I want to achieve it?

How can I best achieve it?

Reflections

Date : _____

 S M T W T F S

Emotional Level

- Happy - Peaceful - Relaxed - Energetic - Satisfied - Disappointed - Lethargic - Tensed - Worried - Unhappy -

Things to be grateful for

Today's happiest moments or memories

Today's achievements, or progress

People I am grateful for

Today's quote or best lesson

Tomorrow's goals

Why do I want to achieve it?

How can I best achieve it?

Reflections

Date : _____

S M T W T F S

Emotional Level

- Happy - Peaceful - Relaxed - Energetic - Satisfied - Disappointed - Lethargic - Tensed - Worried - Unhappy - _____

Things to be grateful for

Today's happiest moments or memories

Today's achievements, or progress

People I am grateful for

Today's quote or best lesson

Tomorrow's goals

Why do I want to achieve it?

How can I best achieve it?

Reflections

Date : _____

 S M T W T F S

Emotional Level

- Happy - Peaceful - Relaxed - Energetic - Satisfied - Disappointed - Lethargic - Tensed - Worried - Unhappy -

Things to be grateful for

Today's happiest moments or memories

Today's achievements, or progress

People I am grateful for

Today's quote or best lesson

Tomorrow's goals

Why do I want to achieve it?

How can I best achieve it?

Reflections

Date : ....

 S M T W T F S

Emotional Level

- Happy - Peaceful - Relaxed - Energetic - Satisfied - Disappointed - Lethargic - Tensed - Worried - Unhappy - _____

Things to be grateful for

Today's happiest moments or memories

Today's achievements, or progress

People I am grateful for

Today's quote or best lesson

Tomorrow's goals

Why do I want to achieve it?

How can I best achieve it?

HERO

Reflections

S M T W T F S

Emotional Level

- Happy - Peaceful - Relaxed - Energetic - Satisfied - Disappointed - Lethargic - Tensed - Worried - Unhappy -

Things to be grateful for

Today's happiest moments or memories

Today's achievements, or progress

People I am grateful for

Today's quote or best lesson

Tomorrow's goals

Why do I want to achieve it?

How can I best achieve it?

Reflections

Date : ....

S M T W T F S

Emotional Level

- Happy - Peaceful - Relaxed - Energetic - Satisfied - Disappointed - Lethargic - Tensed - Worried - Unhappy -

Things to be grateful for

Today's happiest moments or memories

Today's achievements, or progress

People I am grateful for

Today's quote or best lesson

Tomorrow's goals

Why do I want to achieve it?

How can I best achieve it?

HERC

Reflections

Date : _____

S M T W T F S

Emotional Level

- Happy - Peaceful - Relaxed - Energetic - Satisfied - Disappointed - Lethargic - Tensed - Worried - Unhappy -

Things to be grateful for

Today's happiest moments or memories

Today's achievements, or progress

People I am grateful for

Today's quote or best lesson

Tomorrow's goals

Why do I want to achieve it?

How can I best achieve it?

Reflections

Date : _____

 S M T W T F S

Emotional Level

- Happy - Peaceful - Relaxed - Energetic - Satisfied - Disappointed - Lethargic - Tensed - Worried - Unhappy - _____

Things to be grateful for

Today's happiest moments or memories

Today's achievements, or progress

People I am grateful for

Today's quote or best lesson

Tomorrow's goals

Why do I want to achieve it?

How can I best achieve it?

HERO

Reflections

Date : _____

S M T W T F S

Emotional Level

_____ - Happy - Peaceful - Relaxed - Energetic - Satisfied - Disappointed - Lethargic - Tensed - Worried - Unhappy -

Things to be grateful for

Today's happiest moments or memories

Today's achievements, or progress

People I am grateful for

Today's quote or best lesson

Tomorrow's goals

Why do I want to achieve it?

How can I best achieve it?

Reflections

 S M T W T F S

Emotional Level

- Happy - Peaceful - Relaxed - Energetic - Satisfied - Disappointed - Lethargic - Tensed - Worried - Unhappy - _____

Things to be grateful for

Today's happiest moments or memories

Today's achievements, or progress

People I am grateful for

Today's quote or best lesson

Tomorrow's goals

Why do I want to achieve it?

How can I best achieve it?

HERO

Reflections

Date : _____

Emotional Level

_____ - Happy - Peaceful - Relaxed - Energetic - Satisfied - Disappointed - Lethargic - Tensed - Worried - Unhappy - _____

Things to be grateful for

Today's happiest moments or memories

Today's achievements, or progress

People I am grateful for

Today's quote or best lesson

Tomorrow's goals

Why do I want to achieve it?

How can I best achieve it?

Reflections

Date : ....

S M T W T F S

Emotional Level

- Happy - Peaceful - Relaxed - Energetic - Satisfied - Disappointed - Lethargic - Tensed - Worried - Unhappy - ....

Things to be grateful for

Today's happiest moments or memories

Today's achievements, or progress

People I am grateful for

Today's quote or best lesson

Tomorrow's goals

Why do I want to achieve it?

How can I best achieve it?

HERO

Reflections

Date : _____

 S M T W T F S

Emotional Level

_____ - Happy - Peaceful - Relaxed - Energetic - Satisfied - Disappointed - Lethargic - Tensed - Worried - Unhappy - _____

Things to be grateful for

Today's happiest moments or memories

Today's achievements, or progress

People I am grateful for

Today's quote or best lesson

Tomorrow's goals

Why do I want to achieve it?

How can I best achieve it?

HERO

Reflections

Date : ....

S M T W T F S

Emotional Level

- Happy - Peaceful - Relaxed - Energetic - Satisfied - Disappointed - Lethargic - Tensed - Worried - Unhappy -

Things to be grateful for

Today's happiest moments or memories

Today's achievements, or progress

People I am grateful for

Today's quote or best lesson

Tomorrow's goals

Why do I want to achieve it?

How can I best achieve it?

Reflections

Date : _____

 S M T W T F S

Emotional Level

- Happy - Peaceful - Relaxed - Energetic - Satisfied - Disappointed - Lethargic - Tensed - Worried - Unhappy -

Things to be grateful for

Today's happiest moments or memories

Today's achievements, or progress

People I am grateful for

Today's quote or best lesson

Tomorrow's goals

Why do I want to achieve it?

How can I best achieve it?

Reflections

Date : ....

  S M T W T F S

Emotional Level

- Happy - Peaceful - Relaxed - Energetic - Satisfied - Disappointed - Lethargic - Tensed - Worried - Unhappy -

Things to be grateful for

Today's happiest moments or memories

Today's achievements, or progress

People I am grateful for

Today's quote or best lesson

Tomorrow's goals

Why do I want to achieve it?

How can I best achieve it?

Reflections

Date : ....

Emotional Level

- Happy - Peaceful - Relaxed - Energetic - Satisfied - Disappointed - Lethargic - Tensed - Worried - Unhappy -

Things to be grateful for

Today's happiest moments or memories

Today's achievements, or progress

People I am grateful for

Today's quote or best lesson

Tomorrow's goals

Why do I want to achieve it?

How can I best achieve it?

Reflections

Date : ....

  S M T W T F S

Emotional Level

- Happy - Peaceful - Relaxed - Energetic - Satisfied - Disappointed - Lethargic - Tensed - Worried - Unhappy -

Things to be grateful for

Today's happiest moments or memories

Today's achievements, or progress

People I am grateful for

Today's quote or best lesson

Tomorrow's goals

Why do I want to achieve it?

How can I best achieve it?

Reflections

Date : ....

Emotional Level

- Happy - Peaceful - Relaxed - Energetic - Satisfied - Disappointed - Lethargic - Tensed - Worried - Unhappy -

Things to be grateful for

Today's happiest moments or memories

Today's achievements, or progress

People I am grateful for

Today's quote or best lesson

Tomorrow's goals

Why do I want to achieve it?

How can I best achieve it?

Reflections

Date : _____

S M T W T F S

Emotional Level

- Happy - Peaceful - Relaxed - Energetic - Satisfied - Disappointed - Lethargic - Tensed - Worried - Unhappy -

Things to be grateful for

Today's happiest moments or memories

Today's achievements, or progress

People I am grateful for

Today's quote or best lesson

Tomorrow's goals   **Why do I want to achieve it?**

How can I best achieve it?

HERO

Reflections

Date : _____

S M T W T F S

Emotional Level

- Happy - Peaceful - Relaxed - Energetic - Satisfied - Disappointed - Lethargic - Tensed - Worried - Unhappy -

Things to be grateful for

Today's happiest moments or memories

Today's achievements, or progress

People I am grateful for

Today's quote or best lesson

Tomorrow's goals

Why do I want to achieve it?

How can I best achieve it?

Reflections

Date : ....

 S M T W T F S

Emotional Level

_____ - Happy - Peaceful - Relaxed - Energetic - Satisfied - Disappointed - Lethargic - Tensed - Worried - Unhappy - _____

Things to be grateful for

Today's happiest moments or memories

Today's achievements, or progress

People I am grateful for

Today's quote or best lesson

Tomorrow's goals

Why do I want to achieve it?

How can I best achieve it?

HERO

Reflections

Emotional Level

- Happy - Peaceful - Relaxed - Energetic - Satisfied - Disappointed - Lethargic - Tensed - Worried - Unhappy -

Things to be grateful for

Today's happiest moments or memories

Today's achievements, or progress

People I am grateful for

Today's quote or best lesson

Tomorrow's goals

Why do I want to achieve it?

How can I best achieve it?

Reflections

Date : ....

S   M   T   W   T   F   S

Emotional Level

_____ - Happy - Peaceful - Relaxed - Energetic - Satisfied - Disappointed - Lethargic - Tensed - Worried - Unhappy - _____

Things to be grateful for

Today's happiest moments or memories

Today's achievements, or progress

People I am grateful for

Today's quote or best lesson

Tomorrow's goals

Why do I want to achieve it?

How can I best achieve it?

Reflections

Date : _____

S M T W T F S

Emotional Level

- Happy - Peaceful - Relaxed - Energetic - Satisfied - Disappointed - Lethargic - Tensed - Worried - Unhappy -

Things to be grateful for

Today's happiest moments or memories

Today's achievements, or progress

People I am grateful for

Today's quote or best lesson

Tomorrow's goals

Why do I want to achieve it?

How can I best achieve it?

Reflections

Date : ....

 S M T W T F S

Emotional Level

- Happy - Peaceful - Relaxed - Energetic - Satisfied - Disappointed - Lethargic - Tensed - Worried - Unhappy -

Things to be grateful for

Today's happiest moments or memories

Today's achievements, or progress

People I am grateful for

Today's quote or best lesson

Tomorrow's goals

Why do I want to achieve it?

How can I best achieve it?

Reflections

Date : ....

S M T W T F S

Emotional Level

- Happy - Peaceful - Relaxed - Energetic - Satisfied - Disappointed - Lethargic - Tensed - Worried - Unhappy -

Things to be grateful for

Today's happiest moments or memories

Today's achievements, or progress

People I am grateful for

Today's quote or best lesson

Tomorrow's goals

Why do I want to achieve it?

How can I best achieve it?

Reflections

Date : _____

S M T W T F S

Emotional Level

_____ - Happy - Peaceful - Relaxed - Energetic - Satisfied - Disappointed - Lethargic - Tensed - Worried - Unhappy - _____

Things to be grateful for

Today's happiest moments or memories

Today's achievements, or progress

People I am grateful for

Today's quote or best lesson

Tomorrow's goals

Why do I want to achieve it?

How can I best achieve it?

Reflections

Date : _____

S M T W T F S

Emotional Level

- Happy - Peaceful - Relaxed - Energetic - Satisfied - Disappointed - Lethargic - Tensed - Worried - Unhappy -

Things to be grateful for

Today's happiest moments or memories

Today's achievements, or progress

People I am grateful for

Today's quote or best lesson

Tomorrow's goals

Why do I want to achieve it?

How can I best achieve it?

Reflections

Date : ....

Emotional Level

_____ - Happy - Peaceful - Relaxed - Energetic - Satisfied - Disappointed - Lethargic - Tensed - Worried - Unhappy - _____

Things to be grateful for

Today's happiest moments or memories

Today's achievements, or progress

People I am grateful for

Today's quote or best lesson

Tomorrow's goals

Why do I want to achieve it?

How can I best achieve it?

Reflections

Date : ....

 S M T W T F S

Emotional Level

- Happy - Peaceful - Relaxed - Energetic - Satisfied - Disappointed - Lethargic - Tensed - Worried - Unhappy -

Things to be grateful for

Today's happiest moments or memories

Today's achievements, or progress

People I am grateful for

Today's quote or best lesson

Tomorrow's goals

Why do I want to achieve it?

How can I best achieve it?

Reflections

Emotional Level

- Happy - Peaceful - Relaxed - Energetic - Satisfied - Disappointed - Lethargic - Tensed - Worried - Unhappy - _____

Things to be grateful for

Today's happiest moments or memories

Today's achievements, or progress

People I am grateful for

Today's quote or best lesson

Tomorrow's goals

Why do I want to achieve it?

How can I best achieve it?

Reflections

Date : ....

 S M T W T F S

Emotional Level

- Happy - Peaceful - Relaxed - Energetic - Satisfied - Disappointed - Lethargic - Tensed - Worried - Unhappy -

Things to be grateful for

Today's happiest moments or memories

Today's achievements, or progress

People I am grateful for

Today's quote or best lesson

Tomorrow's goals

Why do I want to achieve it?

How can I best achieve it?

Reflections

Date : _____

S M T W T F S

Emotional Level

- Happy - Peaceful - Relaxed - Energetic - Satisfied - Disappointed - Lethargic - Tensed - Worried - Unhappy -

Things to be grateful for

Today's happiest moments or memories

Today's achievements, or progress

People I am grateful for

Today's quote or best lesson

Tomorrow's goals

Why do I want to achieve it?

How can I best achieve it?

HERO

Reflections

Date : ....

S M T W T F S

Emotional Level

_____ - Happy - Peaceful - Relaxed - Energetic - Satisfied - Disappointed - Lethargic - Tensed - Worried - Unhappy - _____

Things to be grateful for

Today's happiest moments or memories

Today's achievements, or progress

People I am grateful for

Today's quote or best lesson

Tomorrow's goals

Why do I want to achieve it?

How can I best achieve it?

Reflections

Date : ....

S M T W T F S

Emotional Level

- Happy - Peaceful - Relaxed - Energetic - Satisfied - Disappointed - Lethargic - Tensed - Worried - Unhappy -

Things to be grateful for

Today's happiest moments or memories

Today's achievements, or progress

People I am grateful for

Today's quote or best lesson

Tomorrow's goals

Why do I want to achieve it?

How can I best achieve it?

Reflections

Date : _____

S   M   T   W   T   F   S

Emotional Level

_____ - Happy - Peaceful - Relaxed - Energetic - Satisfied - Disappointed - Lethargic - Tensed - Worried - Unhappy - _____

Things to be grateful for

Today's happiest moments or memories

Today's achievements, or progress

People I am grateful for

Today's quote or best lesson

Tomorrow's goals

Why do I want to achieve it?

How can I best achieve it?

Reflections

Date : _____

Emotional Level

- Happy - Peaceful - Relaxed - Energetic - Satisfied - Disappointed - Lethargic - Tensed - Worried - Unhappy -

Things to be grateful for

Today's happiest moments or memories

Today's achievements, or progress

People I am grateful for

Today's quote or best lesson

Tomorrow's goals

Why do I want to achieve it?

How can I best achieve it?

Reflections

Date : _____

 S M T W T F S

Emotional Level

- Happy - Peaceful - Relaxed - Energetic - Satisfied - Disappointed - Lethargic - Tensed - Worried - Unhappy -

Things to be grateful for

Today's happiest moments or memories

Today's achievements, or progress

People I am grateful for

Today's quote or best lesson

Tomorrow's goals

Why do I want to achieve it?

 **How can I best achieve it?**

Reflections

Date : ....

S M T W T F S

Emotional Level

_____ - Happy - Peaceful - Relaxed - Energetic - Satisfied - Disappointed - Lethargic - Tensed - Worried - Unhappy - _____

Things to be grateful for

Today's happiest moments or memories

Today's achievements, or progress

People I am grateful for

Today's quote or best lesson

Tomorrow's goals

Why do I want to achieve it?

How can I best achieve it?

HERO

Reflections

 S M T W T F S

Emotional Level

- Happy - Peaceful - Relaxed - Energetic - Satisfied - Disappointed - Lethargic - Tensed - Worried - Unhappy -

Things to be grateful for

Today's happiest moments or memories

Today's achievements, or progress

People I am grateful for

Today's quote or best lesson

Tomorrow's goals

Why do I want to achieve it?

How can I best achieve it?

Reflections

Date : ....

 (S) (M) (T) (W) (T) (F) (S)

Emotional Level

_____ - Happy - Peaceful - Relaxed - Energetic - Satisfied - Disappointed - Lethargic - Tensed - Worried - Unhappy - _____

Things to be grateful for

Today's happiest moments or memories

Today's achievements, or progress

People I am grateful for

Today's quote or best lesson

Tomorrow's goals

Why do I want to achieve it?

How can I best achieve it?

HERC

Reflections

Date : _____

 S M T W T F S

Emotional Level

- Happy - Peaceful - Relaxed - Energetic - Satisfied - Disappointed - Lethargic - Tensed - Worried - Unhappy -

Things to be grateful for

Today's happiest moments or memories

Today's achievements, or progress

People I am grateful for

Today's quote or best lesson

Tomorrow's goals

Why do I want to achieve it?

How can I best achieve it?

Reflections

Date : ....

  (S) (M) (T) (W) (T) (F) (S)

Emotional Level

- Happy - Peaceful - Relaxed - Energetic - Satisfied - Disappointed - Lethargic - Tensed - Worried - Unhappy - ....

Things to be grateful for

Today's happiest moments or memories

Today's achievements, or progress

People I am grateful for

Today's quote or best lesson

Tomorrow's goals   **Why do I want to achieve it?**

How can I best achieve it?

Reflections

Date : _____

Emotional Level

_____ - Happy - Peaceful - Relaxed - Energetic - Satisfied - Disappointed - Lethargic - Tensed - Worried - Unhappy - _____

Things to be grateful for

Today's happiest moments or memories

Today's achievements, or progress

People I am grateful for

Today's quote or best lesson

Tomorrow's goals

Why do I want to achieve it?

How can I best achieve it?

Reflections

Date : _____

 S M T W T F S

Emotional Level

- Happy - Peaceful - Relaxed - Energetic - Satisfied - Disappointed - Lethargic - Tensed - Worried - Unhappy - _____

Things to be grateful for

Today's happiest moments or memories

Today's achievements, or progress

People I am grateful for

Today's quote or best lesson

Tomorrow's goals

Why do I want to achieve it?

How can I best achieve it?

Reflections

Emotional Level

_____ - Happy - Peaceful - Relaxed - Energetic - Satisfied - Disappointed - Lethargic - Tensed - Worried - Unhappy - _____

Things to be grateful for

Today's happiest moments or memories

Today's achievements, or progress

People I am grateful for

Today's quote or best lesson

Tomorrow's goals

Why do I want to achieve it?

How can I best achieve it?

Reflections

Date : ....

S M T W T F S

Emotional Level

.... - Happy - Peaceful - Relaxed - Energetic - Satisfied - Disappointed - Lethargic - Tensed - Worried - Unhappy - ....

Things to be grateful for

Today's happiest moments or memories

Today's achievements, or progress

People I am grateful for

Today's quote or best lesson

Tomorrow's goals

Why do I want to achieve it?

How can I best achieve it?

Reflections

Date : ....

S M T W T F S

Emotional Level

- Happy - Peaceful - Relaxed - Energetic - Satisfied - Disappointed - Lethargic - Tensed - Worried - Unhappy -

Things to be grateful for

Today's happiest moments or memories

Today's achievements, or progress

People I am grateful for

Today's quote or best lesson

Tomorrow's goals

Why do I want to achieve it?

How can I best achieve it?

Reflections

Date : ....

S M T W T F S

Emotional Level

- Happy - Peaceful - Relaxed - Energetic - Satisfied - Disappointed - Lethargic - Tensed - Worried - Unhappy -

Things to be grateful for

Today's happiest moments or memories

Today's achievements, or progress

People I am grateful for

Today's quote or best lesson

Tomorrow's goals

Why do I want to achieve it?

How can I best achieve it?

Reflections

Date : _____

Emotional Level

- Happy - Peaceful - Relaxed - Energetic - Satisfied - Disappointed - Lethargic - Tensed - Worried - Unhappy -

Things to be grateful for

Today's happiest moments or memories

Today's achievements, or progress

People I am grateful for

Today's quote or best lesson

Tomorrow's goals

Why do I want to achieve it?

How can I best achieve it?

Reflections

Date : ....

S M T W T F S

Emotional Level

_____ - Happy - Peaceful - Relaxed - Energetic - Satisfied - Disappointed - Lethargic - Tensed - Worried - Unhappy - _____

Things to be grateful for

Today's happiest moments or memories

Today's achievements, or progress

People I am grateful for

Today's quote or best lesson

Tomorrow's goals

Why do I want to achieve it?

How can I best achieve it?

HERO

Reflections

Date : _____

Emotional Level

_____ - Happy - Peaceful - Relaxed - Energetic - Satisfied - Disappointed - Lethargic - Tensed - Worried - Unhappy - _____

Things to be grateful for

Today's happiest moments or memories

Today's achievements, or progress

People I am grateful for

Today's quote or best lesson

Tomorrow's goals

Why do I want to achieve it?

How can I best achieve it?

Reflections

Date : _____

Emotional Level

_____ - Happy - Peaceful - Relaxed - Energetic - Satisfied - Disappointed - Lethargic - Tensed - Worried - Unhappy - _____

Things to be grateful for

Today's happiest moments or memories

Today's achievements, or progress

People I am grateful for

Today's quote or best lesson

Tomorrow's goals

Why do I want to achieve it?

How can I best achieve it?

Reflections

Date : _____

Emotional Level

- Happy - Peaceful - Relaxed - Energetic - Satisfied - Disappointed - Lethargic - Tensed - Worried - Unhappy -

Things to be grateful for

Today's happiest moments or memories

Today's achievements, or progress

People I am grateful for

Today's quote or best lesson

Tomorrow's goals

Why do I want to achieve it?

How can I best achieve it?

Reflections

Date : ....

Emotional Level

- Happy - Peaceful - Relaxed - Energetic - Satisfied - Disappointed - Lethargic - Tensed - Worried - Unhappy -

Things to be grateful for

Today's happiest moments or memories

Today's achievements, or progress

People I am grateful for

Today's quote or best lesson

Tomorrow's goals

Why do I want to achieve it?

How can I best achieve it?

HERO

Reflections

Date : _____

 S M T W T F S

Emotional Level

_____ - Happy - Peaceful - Relaxed - Energetic - Satisfied - Disappointed - Lethargic - Tensed - Worried - Unhappy - _____

Things to be grateful for

Today's happiest moments or memories

Today's achievements, or progress

People I am grateful for

Today's quote or best lesson

Tomorrow's goals

Why do I want to achieve it?

How can I best achieve it?

HERO

Reflections

Date : ....

Emotional Level

- Happy - Peaceful - Relaxed - Energetic - Satisfied - Disappointed - Lethargic - Tensed - Worried - Unhappy - _____

Things to be grateful for

Today's happiest moments or memories

Today's achievements, or progress

People I am grateful for

Today's quote or best lesson

Tomorrow's goals

Why do I want to achieve it?

How can I best achieve it?

Reflections

Date : _____

S M T W T F S

Emotional Level

- Happy - Peaceful - Relaxed - Energetic - Satisfied - Disappointed - Lethargic - Tensed - Worried - Unhappy -

Things to be grateful for

Today's happiest moments or memories

Today's achievements, or progress

People I am grateful for

Today's quote or best lesson

Tomorrow's goals

Why do I want to achieve it?

How can I best achieve it?

Reflections

Date : ....

S M T W T F S

Emotional Level

- Happy - Peaceful - Relaxed - Energetic - Satisfied - Disappointed - Lethargic - Tensed - Worried - Unhappy -

Things to be grateful for

Today's happiest moments or memories

Today's achievements, or progress

People I am grateful for

Today's quote or best lesson

Tomorrow's goals

Why do I want to achieve it?

How can I best achieve it?

HERO

Reflections

Date : _____

S M T W T F S

Emotional Level

- Happy - Peaceful - Relaxed - Energetic - Satisfied - Disappointed - Lethargic - Tensed - Worried - Unhappy -

Things to be grateful for

Today's happiest moments or memories

Today's achievements, or progress

People I am grateful for

Today's quote or best lesson

Tomorrow's goals

Why do I want to achieve it?

How can I best achieve it?

Reflections

Date : ....

Emotional Level

- Happy - Peaceful - Relaxed - Energetic - Satisfied - Disappointed - Lethargic - Tensed - Worried - Unhappy -

Things to be grateful for

Today's happiest moments or memories

Today's achievements, or progress

People I am grateful for

Today's quote or best lesson

Tomorrow's goals

Why do I want to achieve it?

How can I best achieve it?

YOUR JOURNEY HAS JUST BEGUN. UNLOCK THE CODE.

THE COMPLETE BE A HERO BOOK IS NOW AVAILABLE!

VISIT: WWW.BEAHERO.WORLD BOOK SECTION
OR SEARCH "BE A HERO" ON ONLINE STORES.
FULL COLOR PAPERBACK,
E-BOOK, KINDLE.

YOUR PATH FORWARD ISN'T JUST ABOUT READING.
IT'S ABOUT RISING. KEEP GOING. KEEP GROWING.
BECOME THE HERO YOU WERE BORN TO BE.

HERO

www.ingramcontent.com/pod-product-compliance
Lightning Source LLC
Chambersburg PA
CBHW071106120626
46546CB00003B/1288